UNVEIL

A Guide for the Voiceless

10 STEPS USED TO SURVIVE AND MOVE BEYOND DOMESTIC VIOLENCE

S.H.E. PUBLISHING, LLC

by Latosha Denise

Copyright © 2021 by Latosha Denise.

All rights reserved. Printed in the United States of America. No part of this book may be used or reproduced in any manner whatsoever without written permission except in the case of brief quotations em-bodied in critical articles or reviews.

For information contact: info@shepublishingllc.com
www.shepublishingllc.com

Cover design by Andre Anderson of GodzRoqk Designs

ISBNs:
978-1-953163-08-0
978-1-953163-05-9
978-1-953163-06-6
978-1-953163-07-3

First Edition: March 2021

10 9 8 7 6 5 4 3 2 1

My grandmother's values included not believing in sitting in an emergency room or buying over-the-counter medication. She used home remedies and prayer for medical healing, no trips to the doctor's office, and no antibiotics. She only used southern-style remedies learned from her mother and grandmother to heal fevers, earaches, and sore throats. And from her, I've learned to use my American-style remedies to heal and mend my broken heart. For this reason, I've dedicated this book to her; Bernice Barnes.

Thank you for being the inspiration for my home remedies of healing, the ten steps to finding my voice again.

CONTENTS

INTRODUCTION 1

WHAT IS UNVEIL? 5

THE SHORT STORY 9

    STEP 1 – FINDING FREEDOM IN FORGIVING 21

    STEP 2 - REPOSSESSION 29

    STEP 3 - EVICTION 35

    STEP 4 – FIERCE, FORCE, AND FLAMES 41

    STEP 5 – BROKEN CUFF 47

    STEP 6 – FINDING MY LIFE WITHOUT LOVE IN IT 53

    STEP 7 – STANDING IN THE SHOES ON INDEPENDENCE 59

    STEP 8 – CONNECTING THE STEPS 65

    STEP 9 – MASTER PLAN 73

    STEP 10 – SILENCE IS POWER 77

ACKNOWLEDGEMENTS 85

ABOUT THE AUTHOR 89

"From Misery to Ministry, Tragedy to Triumph, I survived Domestic Violence Abuse. I did not allow myself to become a victim of circumstance. I decided to change the dynamics of my surroundings and became victorious. The chains were broken, and I entered into my freedom. My progress was a process, **But God!!!**"

I Survived Domestic Violence:
Latosha Denise Barnes-Henderson

Introduction

Have you ever wondered where you truly come from, what's your purpose in life on earth, or maybe who your ancestors or descendants are? I did. I constantly wondered why God chose me for this body, for this life, the color of my eyes, the length of my hair and the trials & experiences that life brought my way.

As I began to think of ways to be creative in my writing, I thought of my history, my roots and how it all began decades ago with God's creation of Man and Woman, Adam and Eve, who brought forth Noah, from which we are all descendants. Once God

LATOSHA DENISE

saw that this was good, Noah's generation continued to multiply thousands of years later, creating my parents, Edward and Patricia. Out of this conception, a beautiful vessel was conceived. The date was March 4th, 1972, at 6:04 a.m. This intimacy produced the author of *UN**VEIL**: 10 Steps Used to Survive and Move Beyond Domestic Violence (A Guide for the Voiceless)*.

Born to parents young in age, by the time I was six weeks into life, I began receiving nourishment, love and discipline from my maternal grandmother, who brought forth many wonders of life. My grandmother, a God-fearing woman, introduced me to a church where I met the Lord through Bible readings, lengthy sermons, services and Easter speeches.

As a delicate child with low ferritin levels, fragile weight and tonsil issues, I made frequent visits to two popular clinics in my hometown of Harvey, Illinois. Because of frequent throat infections, my tonsils were eventually removed. Living blocks from the neighborhood elementary school that I could not attend due to late registration, I was bussed to Garfield Elementary School in a nearby town, where I began kindergarten.

Struggling to make ends meet, my grandmother frequently prepared every form of bean imaginable for dinner. While she worked as an elementary school lunchroom lady, we often received what would become my favorite leftovers: chocolate milk and frozen lunch dinners. Many times, my aunts and uncles made fried bologna sandwiches, the bologna with the red plastic around it. They also prepared grilled cheese, which never melted due to the thickness of the government bread we received. These were quick meals to eat until momma arrived home or went grocery shopping. *Those were the days.*

My grandmother, Mother Bernice Barnes, retired to her grave in October 2008, leaving a legacy in her honor, her first granddaughter and grandchild, Latosha Denise. While I still struggled to comprehend that my grandmother's beautiful soul was no longer with us, her wise words, talents, love, kind spirit and great memories lived within me.

What Is UNVEIL?

When I saw the image of writing this book, I did not have a clue where to begin. I was told to just start writing. My thoughts were all over my mind, with so much content that I wanted to cover. After much prayer, I said, *"Self, why not share with the readers, the steps taken on how you survived years of trauma and near-death experiences with domestic violence?"* This inspired me to write. This is how it began. These are the pages of my life, and this is UNVEIL.

I pray that the contents of this book help a victim that is currently experiencing domestic violence abuse. I pray this book lifts the eyes of a surviving victim, who moves beyond abuse, and never looks back. I hope these steps save a mother and child from being disrespected by abuse; I further hope it helps them to escape, heal and pay it forward by helping another victim. This is UN**VEIL**.

Why the title UN**VEIL**, you ask? I am unveiling how I suffered from domestic violence abuse while being married for fifteen years. The cover displays an image of a wedding veil partially uncovered, ripping the mask under the shield of pain, deception, infidelity, body blows, external marks, drops of blood, tears and a multitude of emotional suffering. This is UN**VEIL**.

This experience, the ultimate lessons learned and my passion to help other victims live beyond abuse represent the basis of the ten-steps shared within this book. It is my hope that this publication will become a guide to freeing your body and mind from domestic violence abuse and rebuild your life to a new beginning. This is UN**VEIL**.

Look beyond this reading as another biography of one's life, a survival story or how she or he fled from their abuser. Instead, I want to take you on a nonfictional journey while imagining yourself taking these ten steps. By doing so, you will see the difficulty of surviving domestic violence by moving beyond the fear of your abuser into the depths of survival. I will reveal how I left trauma behind and birthed my destiny. This is UN**VEIL**.

UN**VEIL**

The Short Story

As a survivor of domestic violence, I want to introduce you to me, the individual that has endured 15 years of abuse and survived. I was a 20-year-old newlywed to an individual I only knew for six months. Wanting so badly to move out of my grandmother's house with my two tiny toddlers, I fell for the sweet nothings of what I thought was a better life. I hid the hurt, pain and the trauma experienced after the breakup with my high school sweetheart, first love and father of my two daughters (*2 years-old & 2-month-old*), under the guard of a man I'd barely known.

LATOSHA DENISE

Needing to fill a void, wanting to stop my bleeding heart and butterfly stomach, I married into dysfunction. This encounter was the opposite of love. This young marriage came with food stamps but no food, notices of disconnections, evictions and repossessions. I was forced to return to work after two weeks of giving birth to my twin daughters because the rent had to be paid. At this time, I was the only breadwinner in the home, and my situation went from difficult, to worse, to abuse.

It was his frustrations that led to the physical and verbal abuse imposed, which resulted in missed days of both work and family events, to avoid the embarrassment of the bruises. My tolerance level decreased and the refusal to accept continued abuse ended. After repeatedly being abused, I had no one to turn to; therefore, the acceptance of abuse grew into my normal daily behavior. This generational curse had to end. My mother and grandmother experienced abuse, and as a result, seeing how they survived, I figured they were strong enough, so why couldn't I? I continued in the storm until I could no longer tolerate the black eyes and busted lips. I had no more fight in me. In May 2007, after a heated argument over infidelity, a conflict erupted, causing my daughters to engage in the fight that had me face up on the floor while his hands were around my throat.

    Five of my daughters joined in to save my life. They were tired of the abuse. My youngest daughter stared while crying and screaming in fear. I recall daughter number five, who is now in her early twenties, struggle to get off the bathroom floor after my abuser, her biological father, pushed her. He shoved her so hard with his free hand that her head was inches away from shattering into the bathtub; that would have crushed her skull. Because he was so focused on choking me, he began to fight off my other four daughters with one hand around my neck and the other hitting them. Immediately I began to pray. I gained enough strength to fix my eyes on my daughter, holding the back of her head while crying. I saw my other daughters strike him with the trophies they received from being in various sports. I knew I had to survive and put an end to the years I endured abuse. I prayed my way through, and God saw fit to give me enough strength to break free. I gained enough fight in me to get him off of me and save my daughters. That was the day I thought my abuse ended; I thought I was finally free. Although the abuse ended over seven years ago, and the external scars dissipated, the internal scars remained for years until I took one bold move. I forgave him.

    I often struggled with the memories of my past

abuse, which led me to advocate for women and children traumatized and victimized by domestic violence. That further inspired me to write this book and birth Patricia's Place Domestic Violence Shelter. I am truly honored and blessed that you made this purchase and chose to take this journey with me. My goal is to share the steps with individuals who previously or are currently experiencing domestic violence, those who survived to know that they are not alone.

Follow me as I explore ten significant steps and activities on how to express your abuse in silence, move beyond domestic violence and live an abuse-free life. I want to show victims that there is life beyond verbal, physical, emotional, spiritual, financial and mental abuse.

Experiencing any form of trauma is devastating. Many women have already experienced the pain of childbirth, broken hearts and various other forms of affliction over our lifetime. However, who would ever think abuse would come from a person you exchanged vows with, gave your heart to or conceived a child with? Since my last encounter with physical abuse, I discovered that I was never the one to cause his rage. It was his lack of self-confidence, control and his insecurities. In order to overcome this, I find that uncovering your spiritual connection with God and within yourself to forgive can release you from this pain.

I found myself praying for him more than myself, asking God to soften his heart and help him turn from his abusive ways. I finally realized he had an anger problem. Many times, I would begin to pray right as he was balling his fist to hit me. I would mumble a quiet prayer to not feel the pain from the powerful punch or slap I was about to receive, and for God to cover the eyes and ears of my daughters. I know you're scratching your head asking why I chose those prayers. I found that quiet peace within, even though I was in the process of being abused. This inner peace allowed me to endure the pain while the abuse was taking place. When I knew my daughters were safe and out of harm's way, I let my body and mind sink into a mild state of calmness while the 6'3 240 lb. human beast was attacking my defenseless 5'4 160 lb. body, mother to four of his daughters (six daughters in total) and his wife.

I felt as if I was covered under God's umbrella of protection. Although I endured 15 vigorous years of abuse, I knew I could not beat him, so I continued to pray my way through it all. Finding spiritual guidance and peace within my destiny calmed the storm. It was God who threw a blanket over my body and mind as I received the body and facial blows. Although I knew I was being abused, I did not feel any pain during the attack. This unconsiousness is how I knew God's favor was upon me. I endured extensive external bruises, which healed, but the internal scars lingered longer. I have un**veiled**.

Surviving Domestic Violence

Unveil

by Latosha Denise

UNVEIL

A Guide for the Voiceless

10 STEPS USED TO SURVIVE & MOVE BEYOND DOMESTIC VIOLENCE

S.H.E. PUBLISHING, LLC

by Latosha Denise

LATOSHA DENISE

Step 1

Finding Freedom in

FORGIVING

Forgiving a person who has wronged you is a challenging but necessary task. It's a choice to move forward or remain in bondage. My first step in removing the traumatic chains of bondage was to wholeheartedly forgive my abuser, not for the good of him, but for the interest of me. As I stood eye to eye with my abuser, I took the bold and brave step to utter the words, "I forgive you." Suddenly, I felt a relief of freedom throughout my nature.

Advice to you, my reader, through prayer, my children and the constant reminder that while I'm holding malice and hatred in my heart, he wasn't thinking of me. He moved forward in life, and I was unable to move toward my future. Forgiving was a challenging task to phantom, but I needed that closure to move beyond fear. My spirit would be free from the years of abuse, and it came to pass. In an instant, I removed the 15 years of bondage from victim to victorious.

In December 2013, I was awakened by a shining bright light reflecting across my bedroom ceiling that took me to another dimension. God displayed images of three people across my face. One was my ex-abuser. Throughout the duration of that abusive relationship, I knew God was with me. To this day, I believe God was testing my faith to see if I would obey what he had placed within my spirit. I must admit I was reluctant, but he carried me through each setting. God told me to approach my abuser and tell him I forgive him, and eventually, I did.

During January, February and March of 2014, I could feel God with me on different days and hours. I can remember it like it was yesterday. I was preparing my daughters' gift bags for Valentine's Day. I unexpectedly ran out of material, resulting in a trip to a local store to buy more supplies. My youngest daughter came along with me to get the items needed to complete the Valentine's Day surprise. These gifts would be waiting for my daughters, in their rooms, upon their arrival home from school. While in the card aisle where the needed materials were stocked, I heard a familiar laugh.

    I turned to face the sound, and behold, it was him, among other men finding last-minute love cards. Palpitations quickly began, and fear took over my thoughts and heart. I quickly shifted my thoughts to defense mode and began searching for exits to escape. I promptly forgot who had my back. I started praying, and in an instant, God stepped in. He allowed me to press my way through these words that changed my perspective on life. "I forgive you," I said. He replied, "I forgave you a long time ago." The enemy wanted me to lose control and retaliate by reminiscing on the years of abuse. I turned toward him with a smile and said, "I pray God has mercy on your soul," and I walked away. At that moment, I felt a feeling of relief and calmness over my body. God covered me, protected me and wanted to see if I could be trusted with the assignment of forgiveness. I accomplished this goal by never speaking another negative word about my former abuser, nor did I speak of the terrible things he'd done to me. I've been free of those chains ever since.

    Speaking freely about the dangers of domestic violence abuse to women, children and large groups without fear, crying or anger, I finally realized I was delaying releasing the barriers of my pain. All I had to do was trust God and walk boldly into my freedom. I read a quote once that stated, "Success is the sweetest revenge." My current success is a true testimony about choosing to forgive, and seeking personal revenge on my own only created a shield within. It became difficult to chisel. I chose the most effective defense: to be on the winning side. I allowed God to intercede, and this was the first step in my healing process. My spiritual connection with God inspired me to write these steps. I now have a better understanding of how another human can enter into my life and spit on my soul. *I beat Domestic Violence.*

UN**VEIL**

Activity: Using the lines provided below to write down affirmations for you to focus on!

I Choose	I Remain	I Am
Inner Harmony	*Courageous*	*A Survivor*

LATOSHA DENISE

UNVEIL

LATOSHA DENISE

Step 2

REPOSSESSION

When you hear the word repossession, the first thing that comes to mind is a vehicle being removed or taken for nonpayment. However, in another perspective, repossession is the taking back or forfeiting of a signed contract. This step teaches the importance of knowing what was taken and attaining enough strength to get it back. The contract of marriage was null and void several times throughout my years of abuse.

Abandonment, infidelity, and verbal & emotional

abuse were red flags to leave that union. I was struck while pregnant and subjected to name-calling repeatedly. During my abuse, the torment that endured in front of my daughters somehow gave me the courage to reclaim control of my life. I had to repossess my trust, my heart and my human being. Recovering my self-esteem and confidence during the repossession stage was the tool I used to defeat my enemy.

    I relinquished my fear and took control of my life. My dignity, pride, smile, voice, laughter and walk with God, family, my daughters and my overall appearance were abruptly halted. The interruption was a man who felt the only way to communicate was through the cowardly act of committing physical abuse to his wife and the mother of his children. Sharing this step reveals how my happiness was involuntarily snatched from my possession, but also reveals how I could obtain it again. It was up to me to recover when my abuser possessed my life down to the pit of unbelief. I chose to rescue what was mine. I decided to live. *I beat Domestic Violence.*

UN**VEIL**

Activity: Answer the below questions on the lines provided on the following page.

1. What feelings were oppressed that you can repossess?
2. How long did you hold on before finally relinquishing your fear?
3. What emotions did you have when you were finally set free?
4. Where are you in the process of forgiving your abuser?

LATOSHA DENISE

UNVEIL

LATOSHA DENISE

Step 3

EVICTION

Imagine being a woman trying to extricate yourself from an abusive relationship. This step sounds outrageous, I know, but it is the most difficult stage to conquer. It's unconscionable for a woman to transform her entire frame of mind away from abuse, and the abuser, to focus on anything but surviving. Terminating tenancy occurs when the abuser ends the relationship agreement at the first domestic contact. This stage is when the mind asks the abused to vacate the rental unit. During this step, I had to learn to build the courage to leave because my mind, body and soul were violated by the fist and open hand of a man. During this eviction process, frequently, the hard blow to my face and other body parts felt as if my entire nervous system died.

Taking back what was abruptly stolen allowed me to regain my sense of self-worth and fight to live for me, my children and the ability to share my testimony. Eviction of my soul caused me to lash out at others, lose self-respect and forcefully declare resentment on others. Surviving the eviction stage had much to do with my strong mindset and will to fight. I had to live for my character, self-esteem, dignity and victory. *I beat Domestic Violence.*

UN**VEIL**

Activity: Answer the below questions on the lines provided on the following page.

1. What was taken from you?
2. Did you stay in the relationship long and why?
3. What was your breaking point?
4. What would cause you to return?

LATOSHA DENISE

UNVEIL

LATOSHA DENISE

Step 4

Fierce, Force and

FLAMES

Before Beyoncé, I used to call myself Tosha Fierce due to my unique personality and my will to live. I've always been a feisty female, bold and unafraid to speak up regarding things I saw wrong. I was told that as a young adult growing up, I was aggressive. I fought battles, and I was a savage, demanding and to-the-point. However, even with these labels, which I never agreed upon, domestic violence still showed its ugliness in my life as a young woman.

Three months into my marriage, the abuse began, and I felt persuaded to accept his behavior due to the lack of family support. I can recall walking 15 blocks after being abused. It was late in the evening. I was pregnant with my twins, while my two-year-old held on to the stroller while pushing my 6-month-old daughter. I ended up at my childhood household, my grandmother's home. I was hot and exhausted, only for her to tell me I can stay one night. She said that my children and I had to return home the next morning to my abuser. For the life of me, I could not understand why she would send me back to the house I shared with my in-laws and my abuser. This step is called Fierce. The lack of family support caused a negative relationship to pour over into my immediate family affairs. I did not understand why I was not receiving adequate support from my relatives, to discover many experienced past domestic violence themselves and did not know how to assist me with my trauma. Shortly after returning to my in-laws, and while pregnant, I was struck all over my body while his family stared and did nothing.

As the months progressed into years, the intensity of the abuse snowballed into more hits to my body, face and head. The abuse included harsh words that always felt like a blurred fate. This part of my life is called force. Forced to have sex, forced to speak, forced to cook, forced to bear his children and forced to share the same bed, *UGH*!!!

UNVEIL

Time after time, I wanted to throw up in my mouth due to his cigarette smoking and unclean habits. I persevered by taking my mind to another planet, a planet I called flames. My insides were burning as if I swallowed hot coal. I often escaped to planet flames by isolating my mind into a deep conscious that no one could feel but me. This planet took me to a place of anger where I'd see my life play before my eyes of the heated arguments, body pain and name-calling. I had to come up with a plan to leave my abuser. These three F's, fierce, force and flames, helped me survive this stage of abuse, live to testify and help another victim. *I beat Domestic Violence.*

LATOSHA DENISE

Activity: Draw fierce and bold freedom for yourself.

UNVEIL

Word Search

```
C E S T R E N G T H W D I S O L A T I O N F Z
U T O H Z G V Y Z V G O F L A M E S Z N H H E
G T C V M C V F H U I M J M T C B F A A T C P
T E N O U G H V Z F B E G S U D J H L B N I O
R Y A N Z G B X H U R S V D Z A I E S B A T H
K T V O J S T O P K O T R W N L N L I G L S B
Q I L I S S H I A M K I O P I O R P J B P I E
T T A T D E H E W T E C Z S L R E D F G Y S N
A N N A U N K G M S N V F U H T W C O X T S I
P E O M F E N S R E F I I R Q N O J R D E I L
A D I I M R M K I Y X O E V C O P B C F F C T
L I T T Y A R S W U Z L R I W C E V E K A R O
R Q O N T W I Z W L B E C V A B U S E D S A H
H U M I X A L T Q R N N E O C W V Z M Z P N Y
P R E V E N T I O N S C O R L Z K H D H C L H
O E Y C T G A Y M N Y E S E C R U O S E R U A
```

ABUSED	FIERCE	ISOLATION
AWARENESS	FLAMES	NARCISSISTIC
BROKEN	FORCE	POWER
CONTROL	HELP	PREVENTION
DOMESTIC	HOPE	RESOURCES
VIOLENCE	HOTLINE	SAFETY PLAN
EMOTIONAL	IDENTITY	STRENGTH
ENOUGH	INTIMATION	SURVIVOR

Step 5

BROKEN CUFF

Rotator cuff damage from abuse caused a significant void in my life. I was angry at myself because I allowed another individual to break a bone within my body that caused severe pain for years. I was so traumatized and in fear of my abuser. Surviving this step during my abuse involved me refocusing on other things. I attended my daughters' activities: science fairs, sports events, parent/teacher conferences, choir musicals and talent shows. These beautiful distractions temporarily removed my physical being from feeling hurt and pain to a state of happiness and joy.

Being in my daughters' company, I knew they were safe with me, and I was able to remove myself from his presence long enough to plan my departure both physically and mentally. The pain from my rotator cuff injury was less invasive than the domestic violence abuse. Daily, one foot in front of the other allowed me to repair the damage and graduate from this step successfully. The devastation from this pain of being pushed into a wall opened a force inside of me to walk away and never look back. My point of pain from this injury was enough for me. After fifteen years of all forms of abuse, the decision was made. *I beat Domestic Violence.*

Activity: Answer the below questions on the lines provided on the following pages.
1. Did you sustain injuries, and if so, what were they?
2. Are you healed? If so, what steps did you take to heal?
3. What does trust look like to you?
4. What's on the end of your rope?

LATOSHA DENISE

UNVEIL

Step 6

Finding My Life Without
LOVE IN IT

To refrain from developing a sense of hatred towards my abuser, I opted to love and respect myself. Statistics show that it takes a woman 8-10 times to leave her abuser. These facts are accurate. My mind tried numerous times to flee, but my body suffocated and suffered due to multiple pregnancies. I tried to escape the physical, mental and verbal abuse for years, but his manipulative tactics and not-so-charming, sweet nothings forced me to stay. I was at my breaking point. I had endured abuse way past its expiration date and now strong enough to make an intelligent, conscious decision to leave. I allowed this act to enter into my life without love, which displays loving myself enough to leave and save my children. The hidden hope within the walls of inner suffering caused me to become bold in my walk with Christ and life. My head was below my eyes long enough to leave and never return. This was hidden hope I thought was lost forever. My life had been built on faith. *I beat Domestic Violence.*

UNVEIL

Activity: Make a list of ways in which you will/have begun to love yourself in the midst of your storm.

_____

_____

_____

_____

_____

_____

_____

LATOSHA DENISE

UNVEIL

Step 7

Standing in the Shoes of
INDEPENDENCE

Anyone who knows me knows I am a lover of shoes of all makes and models. I am the current owner of over one hundred pairs of shoes (mostly heels) that I adore. I have difficulty throwing the ones that are in disarray in the trash. However, some were oftentimes unrepairable. Walking in others' shoes is difficult. Someone once said that one could never understand another's pain unless you've walked in their shoes. Not true. This is a myth. I was one of the individuals that felt my mother's pain as she endured her abuse decades before I began my years of trauma.

At a young age, I witnessed her painful experience and often, it seemed as if I felt the blows and slaps of her disfigured face until it was my experience. During the years of my abuse, I could not understand how I was allowing myself to be abused by someone who was supposed to protect me, but I held on to my faith, stopped trying to meet his approval and began to dress to impress for success. I enrolled in a local community college and have been receiving my education ever since. Now I am the proud owner of two Master's degrees and a multitude of certifications. It became me, myself and I, along with six beautiful sunflowers. *I beat Domestic Violence.*

Activity: This point in my life was the beginning of a new groundbreaking where *I* along with the work of being better, birthed. I ask you the following questions:

1. Where have your shoes taken you?
2. Whose shoes are you wearing?
3. Why are you allowing yourself to wear these shoes?
4. Do you repair or destroy damaged shoes?

LATOSHA DENISE

UNVEIL

LATOSHA DENISE

Step 8

Connecting the

STEPS

Abuse is the misuse of power and control. The violation of one's trust frequently develops into the difficulty of understanding 'WHY me'. The threats, intimidation and isolation became a repetitive process during my years of suffering. However, with the look on my daughter's face and feeling the exhaustion of fear of my mind and body, I realized I am a queen of the Most High. So I began connecting the dots to understand how I entered into this space, and discover the steps I needed to execute and depart.

First, I had to acknowledge that I was a victim. I did not ask to be abused, nor was it my fault. Next, I had to accept that his behavior would not change, so I had to cease producing more children and carefully plan me and my children's exit. I created an assessment on my circumstance, which included four levels:

- **Level 1:** regularly seeing the stained marks on my body that I will take to my grave.
- **Level 2:** My princesses played a significant part in my decision to stay or leave. I did not want my daughters to think that all men are abusers, which would deter their ability to love one day. I also did not want my daughters to view me as a weak woman who used to be strong; a vulnerable woman who allowed a man to destroy her character and self-esteem; or a defenseless woman who was too afraid to face her fears.
- **Level 3:** The presence of verbal abuse
- **Level 4:** If I wanted to live or die

Putting these ideals into perspective daily assisted me with creating these levels. My abuser's desire for that power and control was more important than his children, and he wanted me to feel pain and suffering.

So, what's next? I made sure my spiritual connection with God, family and friends was tight and in order. I began to track my money and set self-goals. I prepared my mind never to allow worry and doubt to enter. I reconnected with my inner spirit to trust the process and learn from this experience.

LATOSHA DENISE

Activity: Connect the dots to create a purple ribbon.

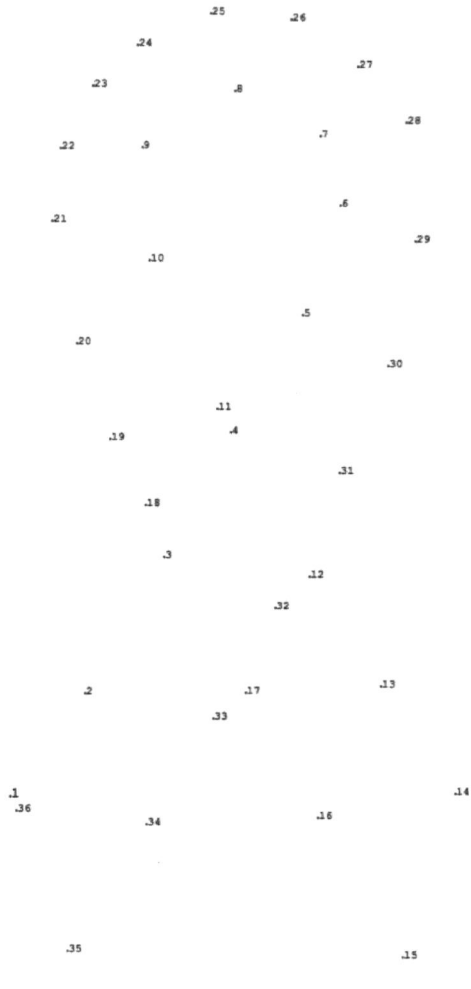

68

Activity: Answer the questions on the lines provided below.

1. What steps have/are you taking to move beyond your abuse?
2. How has your life's journey allowed you to connect with where you are destined to be?
3. What's your meaning of self-care?

_____

_____

_____

_____

_____

_____

LATOSHA DENISE

UNVEIL

LATOSHA DENISE

Step 9

MASTER PLAN

Ignorance begets ignorance. During this time in my life, while dealing and tired of the abuse, I began my plan of escape with my daughters. I was not just leaving my home, but the marriage in its entirety.

Progress is a process. From strength to strength, I started to do what was right and not feel guilty about my happiness. My life was set up like a maze during my abuse. It felt as if I was walking through doors with no exits. During this difficult but necessary step, I was drowning in my misery. I was confused about where I would go with six children and how I would make it out here by myself with no help. I began to bury myself within myself as my mind began to think for me, instead of thinking for myself. I began to feel hopeless, confused about if it was abuse or whether this was just my imagination.

Once I looked over my body and saw the bruises beginning to heal, I started with the daily method of putting one foot in front of the other. I conquered this step by speaking over myself and inserting daily encouragement. I was too busy hiding my pain that I did not know the difference between empathy and emptiness. I transformed into a scared shell and lost myself in translation until these words were uttered into my spirit, saying, "*I am not what happened to me. I am what I chose to become.*"

Instantly, the mask was removed, and I began to see the light in me. This is the beginning of my end, and this is **UNVEIL**. I successfully removed 15 years of abuse and turned those hurtful years into Patricia's Place Domestic Violence Shelter. I further educated myself, and became an advocate for the voiceless. I motivate and empower women & children from all walks of life to break their silence, survive, live purposefully and achieve their goals. I was able to scratch life lessons off my bucket list.

UN**VEIL**

Activity: What is your plan of action? Create your path of power and strength to get out!

Step 10

SILENCE IS
POWER

Often, I found myself by myself to escape the dangers of my abuser. I discovered silence is powerful, and I knew enough was enough. During this stage of my abuse, I found my new happiness while deciding to leave the marriage. I discovered moving in silence is the actual power wheel. I can honestly say I did not know the difference between moving from abuse to abundance. I felt abandoned by God until a still calm overcame my soul, and I let go of shame. I knew at this point; it was time for a change.

LATOSHA DENISE

Specifically, in silence, I saved money, documented every argument, every hit, took pictures of the marks & injuries, searched for new employment opportunities, built my credit, and started educating myself on good nutrition. I even began to start grooming myself better: getting my hair and nails done. I agreed more with his requests and demands for the safety of my children and myself. As a result, I started spending less and less time at home. *I beat Domestic Violence.*

UNVEIL

Activity: How will you begin to move in silience?

LATOSHA DENISE

UNVEIL

LATOSHA DENISE

My Abuse was not in vain. I survived by guarding myself in the spirit to avoid being faithless. Either I was going to stay distracted by my past or focus on my future. Faith, Focus and Follow-through.

I Survived Domestic Violence:
Latosha Denise Barnes-Henderson

ACKNOWLEDGEMENTS

Thankful first and foremost to my heavenly father for trusting me with this assignment and allowing me to soar beyond higher sights. God's plans and purpose for my life were seen by Him while in my mother's womb. His grace, mercy and favor allowed me to seek his assistance and move beyond my fears to turn my dreams into a reality. I am alive today to share my victory only because of God's grace.

To my siblings, aunts & uncles, close friends, church family and staff at Patricia's Place Domestic Violence Shelter-- my deepest gratitude for your continued support. I also give thanks to SHE Publishing, LLC for the time we spent completing this part-memoir, part self-help book and

LATOSHA DENISE

Andre Anderson of GodzRoqk Designs for creating three amazing and meaningful book covers.

To my late grandmother, Bernice Barnes, who encouraged me, pushed me and instilled great values for loving God, family, myself and others, I thank you. My grandmother will always be the woman-to-woman figure who I continue to mimic. From my beginning, she nourished me with love, support and discipline. Her motherly love understood my struggles and allowed me to develop into my own identity.

As a mother of six beautiful queens, I now understand the importance of raising children in a safe, secure and loving environment. Making sure my daughters did not suffer from the worldly struggles that life handed my grandmother, I elected to remove myself from traditional traditions and pursue my path of life, which has been an ultimate success story in my parenting journey. Thank you, Mama, as I often called her; continue resting in power.

To my mother, Patricia, thank you for allowing me to name my shelter in your honor and spread my wings to soar high above. You have always encouraged me and told me how proud you were of me. Anytime I just needed to talk, you were there. When I found myself frustrated, your exact words were "*Let Go and Let God.*"

Special thanks to my six daughters who were patient, understanding and provided much-needed encouragement to pursue my dreams of sharing my testimony with others who have or are currently experiencing domestic violence.

Thank you for blessing me with grandchildren who call me Ma-Ma, giving me space and time to build my vision as I completed my degrees and worked full time. All of you understood this assignment and never hesitated to question why. Thank you, my Diva Queens.

Finally, to my husband, Kevin. My love, protector and my provider. You are my prayer partner and my best friend. Thank you for understanding how vital writing these steps are to me. Thank you for your correction, for sharing the challenges we faced as husband and wife together and for giving me my own identity and freedom to just be me.

ABOUT THE AUTHOR

Latosha Denise Barnes-Henderson was born to the parents of Edward McIntosh and Patricia Ann Barnes in Harvey, Illinois, at Ingalls Memorial Hospital. She is the oldest of six siblings between her mother and father, under which tragic circumstances lead to the death of one of her brothers, only 18 years of age, due to Chicago gun violence in January 2001. Barnes-Henderson has six beautiful daughters: Amber Patrice, Tanea Shirlet, Dominique Renee, Deanna Raquel, Ashley Bernice and Tamiah Michelle.

Barnes-Henderson attended schools in Blue Island, Harvey, Dixmoor, South Holland and University Park; all cities within the State of Illinois. In Barnes-Henderson's lifetime, she has earned her Bachelors in Interdisciplinary Studies,

LATOSHA DENISE

Masters in Criminal Justice and Masters in Addiction Studies.

Advocating for domestic violence victims is an affiliate with Barnes-Henderson's non-for-profit organization where she provides a safe haven for women and children seeking shelter, food, clothing and other supportive services. With that said, she is the Founder and Executive Director of Patricia's Place Domestic Violence Shelter. Barnes-Henderson's hobbies consist of traveling, shopping, letting off some steam at the gun range, hanging with family and friends, fine dining and drinking sweet red wine. She also enjoys going to church, and networking with other like-minded individuals who share the same passion. Barnes-Henderson's future endeavors include:

- Writing more books, and
- Adding more components to Patricia's Place - Domestic Violence Shelter.

Barnes-Henderson is truly a woman of substance, and she is making a difference within the community.

www.ingramcontent.com/pod-product-compliance
Lightning Source LLC
Chambersburg PA
CBHW050740080526
44579CB00018B/122